Indians
of the California
Mission Frontier

Jack S. Williams
Thomas L. Davis

The Rosen Publishing Group's
PowerKids Press™
New York

To the native people who built the missions and to their descendants
who continue to preserve their sacred beliefs and practices

Published in 2004 by The Rosen Publishing Group, Inc.
29 East 21st Street, New York, NY 10010

First Edition

Editor: Joanne Randolph
Book Design: Corinne Jacob

Photo and Illustration Credits: Cover, pp. 25, 29 courtesy of the Bancroft Library, University of California, Berkeley; back cover courtesy of Jack Williams; p. 4 © Marc Muench/CORBIS; pp. 6, 17 North Wind Picture Archives; pp. 8, 20, 30, 33 drawings by Father Ignacio Tirsch, courtesy of the National Library of the Czech Republic; pp. 9, 10 Scala/Art Resource, NY; p. 11 Museo Naval, Madrid; p. 13 © CORBIS; p. 14 68-56-1-2: "Father Serra Celebrates Mass at Monterey," Leon Trousset, Oil on Canvas, 1876, California Historical Society Fine Arts Collection; p. 18 Réunion des Musées Nationaux/Art Resource, NY; p. 22 courtesy of the Albinger Archeological Museum, City of Ventura, CA, photo © Cristina Taccone; pp. 23, 32, 34 courtesy of Ventura County Museum of History & Art, background painting on p. 23 courtesy of Kent Christenson, photos © Cristina Taccone; p. 37 illustrated by Jack Williams; p. 38 courtesy Mission San Luis Obispo, Dalidio Collection, photo © Cristina Taccone; p. 40 courtesy of Mission San Antonio, photo © Cristina Taccone p. 43 courtesy of University of Southern California, on behalf of the USC Specialized Libraries and Archival Collections; p. 46 © 2002 Geoatlas; p. 50 Arizona Historical Society—Yuma; p. 52 courtesy of the California History Room, California State Library, Sacramento, California; p. 55 courtesy of Santa Barbara Mission Archive—Library, reproduction photo © Cristina Taccone; p. 57 original art reference by Jack Williams, recreation by Corinne Jacob.

The illustration, shown in part on the cover and here in its entirety, shows Ohlone Indians performing their native dances for a group of foreign visitors to Mission Dolores, near the San Francisco Bay. The padres encouraged the Indians to preserve certain aspects of their cultures, such as the arts. This image was created by Ludovik (Louis) Choris, the artist for the Russian expedition to the North Pacific in 1815–1818. The plate appeared in his atlas.

Williams, Jack S.
Indians of the California mission frontier / Jack S. Williams and Thomas L. Davis.
p. cm.
Includes bibliographical references and index.
Contents: The California frontier—How we know about the mission Indians—The goals of the mission program—The Indians come to the missions—The challenges of mission life—How the missions were organized—The changing patterns of everyday things—Spiritual life—Living on a mission rancho—Non-mission Indian neighbors—Native responses to life at the missions—The mission heritage.
  ISBN 0-8239-6281-4 (lib. bdg.)
1. Indians of North America—Missions—California—Juvenile literature. 2. Missions—California—Juvenile literature. [1. Indians of North America—Missions—California. 2. Missions—California—History. 3. California—History—To 1846.]   I. Davis, Thomas L. II. Title.
  E78.C15W54 2004
  979.4'00497—dc21

                                                                    2002006544

Manufactured in the United States of America

Contents

The California Frontier

The land that would become known as California existed long before any people arrived there. For millions of years, the waves crashed on the rocks and sandy beaches of the coastline without ever being seen by human eyes. Here were mountains that reached into the clouds, forests of towering trees, and grassy plains that seemed to stretch on forever. In the far south, deserts filled with sand dunes and rocks shimmered in summer temperatures that rose above 120°F (48.9°C). Much of the landscape was as desolate and barren as the surface of the moon. The place that would later become known as California was a land with many features. It was also a place of extremes.

No one knows for sure when the first humans came to this region. Most experts believe that sometime between forty thousand and thirteen thousand years ago, people from Asia arrived in North America. After they traveled from Siberia to Alaska across a frozen land bridge, the immigrants slowly moved south. By twelve thousand years ago, the descendants of the first explorers of this vast region had reached the tip of South America.

Some of the first Indian nations that made their home in America eventually settled in California. As time passed, new people who had created communities in adjacent areas moved into the region. Older nations either moved away or united with these newcomers. By two thousand years ago, the

◄ *Waves crash on a sandy beach near growing cacti in Baja California. The coastal environment is just one aspect of California's varied geography.*

The explorer Hernán Cortés (1485–1547), also called Ferdinando, is shown here in this undated, hand-colored engraving. In his explorations of the Pacific coast, he found a land that he called California.

native people of California were as different from one another as the features of the region's landscape. For thousands of years, California's Native Americans lived without ever knowing about the people who existed on the other side of the Atlantic and Pacific Oceans.

The Indian world was changed forever when, in 1492, Christopher Columbus came in search of a new route from Europe to China, but found lands that Europeans had never known existed. Spain soon sent wave after wave of soldier-explorers, called conquistadors, to claim any rich lands that they could find.

Hernán Cortés was one of the most famous explorers. He found people in Central Mexico who were rich beyond the Europeans' wildest dreams. After conquering the Aztec Nation, he began to search for other rich kingdoms. Cortés organized several expeditions to explore the Pacific coast of Mexico.

One of these groups landed on the rocky shores of a place that he called California. Not many people were willing to move to the remote region, which is today a part of modern Baja, or Lower, California. Problems with Indians and droughts soon forced Cortés's colonists to return to Central Mexico.

During the decades that followed, conquistadors led by Juan Rodriguez Cabrillo, Hernando de Alarcón, and Melchor Díaz explored various parts of Upper, or Alta, California. More than two hundred years would pass before any colonists would be sent by a European power to live in Alta California, however.

Between 1600 and 1750, Spanish ships occasionally visited California's shores as they made their way from the Philippines to Mexico. The vessels' crews sometimes stopped to gather supplies, such as water and firewood. We do not have any detailed descriptions about the things that were going on among the Native Americans of California during this period. We know that throughout most of North America and South America, Europeans inadvertently introduced diseases, such as smallpox, that may have killed as many as 95 percent of the Indian people. Given the frequent visits of the explorers and merchants to California, it is likely that many coastal Indian nations suffered terrible losses. Their numbers probably gradually increased during the one hundred and fifty years that followed. A similar pattern of sharp decline and recovery has been recorded for many other native groups that lived in the Americas.

Although they did not send soldiers to occupy the region for more than a hundred years from the time of their first visits, the kings and queens of Spain

Spanish galleons often stopped in California as these ships sailed from the colonies in the Philippines to the colonies in Mexico. In this engraving, the ship is arriving at the San José del Cabo mission in Baja California. In the foreground, settlers are engaged in various activities of mission life, such as farming.

claimed ownership of all of California. During the middle of the eighteenth century, Carlos III, king of Spain, became concerned about English and Russian exploration of the Pacific Ocean. He was afraid that the governments of these countries would send ships to take what he considered his territory. If Alta California was lost, the ports of San Diego and Monterey could be used to attack Mexico and Peru, which were the richest parts of the Spanish Empire.

In 1769, an expedition was launched to conquer Alta California and its Indians. Carlos III wanted to occupy the region, but he did not have the money, the men, or the colonists that he needed. He quickly realized that his only

Carlos III (1716–1788), also called Charles III, is shown here in Francesco Liani's portrait. The king worked hard to protect and expand Spain's empire in the Americas.

hope was to try to create some kind of friendship with the Native Americans.

The Spanish government decided to create missions in order to accomplish the king's objectives. These settlements would be communities in which Indians would gradually become Spanish citizens. In the eyes of the government, a person had to believe in the Roman Catholic religion if he or she wanted to be considered a civilized person. Therefore, the provinces' native nations had to become Christians. In time, the Indians would provide most of the troops who would protect the region. Eventually, the transformed Indian nations would enjoy prosperity, and they might even be able to send taxes to Spain.

Priests from the Franciscan Order were put in charge of the missions. The priests believed that the development of the new Californian frontier would

This fresco of Saint Francis of Assisi, who lived around 1181–1226, was done by Giotto di Bondone. The fresco shows Saint Francis preaching to the birds. He considered all living creatures his "brothers" or his "sisters." Saint Francis gave up his worldly possessions and took on a life of poverty, because he believed that was necessary to lead a religious life.

provide them with a chance to share God and to help people. The priests were also happy to serve the king as loyal representatives of the Spanish Empire. They were certain that they could build mission communities that combined the best features of the European and Native American worlds. If they succeeded, Spanish systems of government and religion would exist alongside the Indians' sense of community and love of nature.

When the Spaniards began to colonize California, they were amazed that the people there spoke so many languages and that the nations were so fiercely independent from one another. The peoples that they found included the Kumeyaay, the Kamia, the Luiseño, the Juaneño, the Tongva, the Chumash, the Salinans, the Esselen, the Ohlone, the Quechan, the Yokuts, the Pomo, the Cahuillas, and the Coast Miwok.

This detail of a sketch of a Native American woman of Monterey was done in the 1700s by José Cardero. The woman is wearing clothing made of both rabbit skins and deerskins.

Spanish government officials realized that the success of the colony relied on the missions and on the cooperation of the Native Americans. Without Indian support, there would never have been missions or a Spanish California.

How We Know About the Mission Indians

Accurate information about California's early missions and Indians is often difficult to find. Researchers are not able to visit the past. To understand what happened in the missions, we gather evidence carefully and put it together, as do detectives. Many different kinds of scholars work in this effort. Archaeologists study the ruins of buildings, broken pieces of pottery, and similar traces of past human behavior. Historians study the written records, the artwork, and the photographs that have been left behind by earlier generations. Cultural anthropologists study the customs of present-day people. Many of the members of modern Indian nations continue traditions that date from hundreds, and even thousands, of years ago. By carefully studying their ways of doing things, cultural anthropologists can sometimes discover evidence that can explain parts of historical documents or artifacts at archaeological sites. The work of cultural anthropologists is especially important for the California missions because almost none of the Indians left written descriptions of their mission experiences.

Grandfather Semu Huate, a religious leader, carries on traditions and ancient customs that are unique to the Chumash of the Santa Bárbara area.

The Stages of the Mission Program

The Franciscans who arrived in California had a master plan for developing missions. The plan had been created over many centuries in other parts of the Americas that Spain had conquered. There were three basic stages through which each mission outpost was expected to go. During the early days, the Indians would live much as they had in the past. Over a decade or more, the missionaries would introduce Christianity and European customs to the Native Americans. During this period, the communities where the Indians lived were called missions, or *misiones*.

When the native people had learned to live as Spanish citizens, the settlements would become *doctrinas*. The Indian leaders there would be given responsibility, personal freedom, and control over their settlements' property.

When the Indians had mastered all the skills that were required of Spanish citizens, the padres, or priests, would prepare to leave. Priests who were not missionaries would be sent to the settlements to provide religious services. Indian leaders would take over the management of the outposts. Those who had lived in what had once been called misiones and then doctrinas, would be considered equal to other Spanish Christians. Thereafter, the community and the settlement in which they lived would be called a curacy. This final transfer of rights and property to the native peoples was called secularization.

◄ *In this 1877 oil painting, artist Leon Trousset imagined what the scene might have looked like when Father Serra dedicated the site of the capital and mission headquarters at Monterey in 1771.*

The Indians Come to the Missions

The Franciscans realized that they had to persuade Indians to live at the missions. There were too few soldiers for the padres to force Native Americans to come stay with them at the missions, and the padres wanted the Native Americans to come because they wanted to learn about God and the Spanish way of life.

Why would a Native American choose to live in a mission? A person who joined one of the new settlements enjoyed a number of practical benefits. The Indians realized that the Spaniards would make good allies if they had to fight a war against other native groups or Europeans. The Franciscans also brought steel knives, axes, new kinds of food, and animals such as horses, sheep, cattle, mules, and chickens. They also had many beautiful customs and objects, including paintings, statues, religious rituals, and powerful music.

Many Indians probably decided to join the missions because of the padres' preaching. The Franciscans were experts at giving persuasive speeches. They stressed the fact that everything that would exist in the new settlements would belong to the native community. They also talked about hell, which may have frightened some younger Native Americans. Often, the padres offered the natives a chance to help create a new kind of society called a utopia. Many Indians had been involved in centuries of fighting with

Franciscans and Native Americans gather for a religious ritual, a mass for the dead, in this 1883 hand-colored engraving by Henry Sandham.

their neighbors, and some came to believe that they could live in harmony with one another, the newcomers, and God. They thought that they could create a place where everyone would be treated fairly, and no one would go hungry or lack a good job.

Indians who decided to move to the missions were known as neophytes, or new followers. The native chiefs often brought whole villages to the new Spanish settlements. Once they had moved, the Indian leaders continued to serve in important roles. The neophytes often visited the Native Americans

In the late 1760s, Alexandre J. Nöel created this drawing of Native Americans in a funeral procession at mission San José in Baja California. The type of brush houses shown were typical of the California missions during their early stages of development.

who did not live at the missions. They sometimes persuaded these people, whom the padres called gentiles, to come to live with them.

As the Franciscan outposts grew larger, the neophytes' sheep, horses, and cattle multiplied. The animals ate the plants that the Indians had grown before the arrival of the Europeans and either damaged or destroyed many other parts of the natural environment. Diseases that were brought to California by the newcomers and were transmitted to the natives killed both the neophytes and the gentiles. New kinds of weapons, such as guns, made it easier for people to hunt animals into extinction. Steel axes made it easier to cut down trees. Throughout the coastal region, it became difficult for the Indians to keep their traditional way of life.

During the early days of the missions, many gentiles ignored the newcomers. Now that they could no longer avoid living with the changes that the Europeans had introduced, some of these Native Americans gave up and moved into the missions. A few Indians managed to live secret lives based on their older customs in the rugged mountains and other hidden places. Other gentiles moved away to live in the Central Valley beyond the influence of the Spaniards.

The Challenges of Mission Life

Once they moved into the missions, Native Americans faced a life that was filled with exciting opportunities as well as difficult challenges. There were many new things and ideas to explore. However, there were also many opportunities for misunderstandings and conflicts.

Life Before the Missions

During the era before the Franciscans arrived, all of the native Californian groups lived in a world that centered on village settlements. Every community was surrounded by territory where its people had the right to hunt and gather food. No one from a different village was allowed to come into these areas without permission. California was made up of hundreds of different village nations. Sometimes these groups were at peace with one another, and sometimes they fought bitter wars.

Every community has some form of social structure. Social structure provides a way to organize people into smaller groups and to assign them appropriate jobs. A person found his or her place in the community based on a number of factors. Among the California Indians, individuals were usually assigned to a group based on whether they were men or women, how old they were, how much wealth they had, what they did to make a

Two Native Americans from Baja California are shown with a deer they have hunted with bows and arrows in this painting by Ignacio Tirsch. Each Native American group had special areas where only they were allowed to hunt.

 21

A plank canoe, or tomol, *such as this modern reproduction, could hold as many as twelve adults. Tomols were also used when fishing and hunting seals, otters, and whales. A tomol was made from wood found on the shore, finished with sharkskin, and held together with milkweed cords. The Chumash used tomols to travel between the Santa Barbara Coast and the Channel Islands.*

living, and who their parents were. In nearly all of California's native communities, the most powerful person was the village leader, sometimes called a chief, who ruled with the help of a team of elders.

Families were the smallest social groups. In many nations, the families were combined into larger groups called clans. Members believed that their founder was an animal, such as a dolphin, a bear, or an eagle. Clans were usually assigned special jobs. In most Californian societies there were also full-time village doctors, religious specialists, singers, and dancers. A few nations had special groups of craftsmen who worked full-time to create canoes or shell beads.

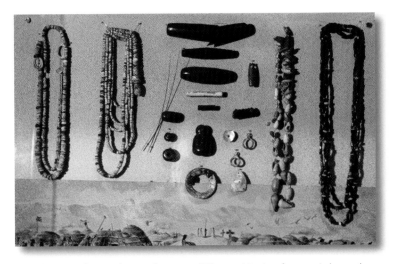

Indian craftspeople used many different kinds of materials, such as bones, shells, and stones, to make jewelry and tools. The items shown here include shell necklaces, stone pipes, jewelry, and fishhooks.

The native nations' religions were very different from one another and were as complex as any of those that are practiced today. Although they were not the same, most Indian religions emphasized respect for animals, land, and other natural resources.

Life throughout California was closely tied to Earth and nature. Most people relied on foods that they could either hunt or gather. Many native nations took steps to encourage some wild plants to grow. This produced additional food, such as acorns and chia seeds, and even helped to increase the population of certain kinds of animals that they liked to eat, such as deer. The Indians developed many amazing methods to manage their food and animal resources. They had many rules that promoted conservation. There were also customs that helped children to understand that they were one small part of a larger natural world.

Despite their attempts to live in peace and harmony with nature, early Indians still faced many problems. Diseases often killed people, plants, and animals. Disastrous storms, droughts, and other catastrophes took place.

Sometimes nations fought over natural resources, such as food and water. The first Californians lived in a world of plenty, but it was also full of hardship, conflict, and sorrow.

The New Patterns of Life in the Missions

Once they moved into the missions, the natives began to enjoy many of the advantages of making friends with the padres. There were trade goods, new foods, and different kinds of rituals and celebrations, as well as opportunities to learn new skills.

The new system of Spanish rule made it possible for Indians to take part in a larger global community. The missionaries taught the Indians about Europe, Asia, South America, and other faraway places and peoples. When the Indians learned to speak Spanish, they were able to communicate with more people.

The missions also offered the Indians the possibility of creating a period of peace and wealth. Because the priests were outsiders, the Indians quickly realized that the Franciscans could settle disputes between rival Indian nations. Many priests were able to create mission communities made up of natives who had always fought each other.

Some of the Indian leaders joined the missions in order to increase their power by becoming Spanish allies. Many received special privileges and gifts of trade goods that they used to become wealthy. Some of these men took advantage of their European allies' military strength to settle old disputes with rival groups. The Spaniards sometimes unknowingly became powerful players in old tribal conflicts.

Although there were many benefits to living at the missions, there were also many problems. At the larger mission settlements, such as Mission Santa Clara, some Native Americans spoke various languages and had

Habitants de Californie.

Louis Choris sketched these faces of San Francisco mission Indians living in the area in 1816. California's Native Americans often wore distinctive hairstyles that identified them as living in a particular village.

different customs. The priests who lived there found it extremely hard to communicate with the neophytes. It was also hard for the Indians to talk with one another. Living so close together meant that they often misunderstood one another, which would lead to fights or arguments.

There can be no doubt that many of the Indians did not like the Franciscans' religious beliefs. The padres often tried to persuade the neophytes to give up their traditions. Most Franciscans felt that the Native Americans would eventually adopt Christianity as the true path to happiness and would give up their older customs. Instead, most Indians added Christian customs to their traditional views and rituals. Many neophytes felt sorry for the missionaries, who could not understand or appreciate the beauty and the truth in the Indians' religious traditions.

The native Californians also suffered from dozens of new diseases. The neophytes could not understand why they were afflicted with such terrible diseases while the newcomers remained healthy. At all the missions except San Luis Rey, more native people died each year than were born. This kind of population loss was seen throughout the Americas. Fortunately, at some point the number of Indians in most regions stopped decreasing.

The reason that natives died more rapidly from diseases such as smallpox was that the Europeans had already been exposed to these illnesses for many centuries. Through a complicated process known as natural selection, people with greater resistance to the diseases had survived and had had children more often than those who had not had a resistance. As a result, a disease that made a European sick would often kill many Indians.

Even if the quality of most people's lives was better at the new missions, the Indians gradually began to understand that parts of the world that they had known and the customs that they had followed would not survive. Many precious things were lost to Native Americans, and this loss created a feeling of hopelessness among many neophytes.

How the Missions Were Organized

When the missionaries arrived in a new region, they liked to gather the Indians together into a single settlement, called a *reducción*. Having the neophytes in one place made it easier for the Franciscans to communicate with and organize the natives. Without a reducción, the padres would have had to travel from village to village, repeating their lessons, religious services, and ceremonies. Because there were thousands of small villages in California, the creation of reducciónes was very important to the missionaries.

The mission reducciónes changed over time. At first, life went on much as it had during earlier periods for the mission Indians. Gradually, the padres tried to persuade native leaders to follow new ways of doing things. The leaders were expected to help the Franciscans communicate the new ways and to serve as examples to their people.

Early on, the padres worked to introduce a new schedule to the Indian people. The mission bells rang to indicate times for prayer, work, meals, and recreation. The chores usually began shortly after sunrise. After a religious service and breakfast, the neophytes went to work. At about noon, everyone ate the main meal of the day. In the early afternoon, people rested or visited with friends. Late in the day, work began again and continued until sunset. This was followed by another church service, followed by the final meal of the day.

José Cardero created this view of Mission Carmel in 1791. Over time, the brush buildings were replaced with more permanent structures made from adobe.

N. 2

m. 1

abildung der kleidung so alle weibliche so wohl Jung als alten in der Mißion in Californien von den Patres bekommen
die sorgt die machte so mit ihrer Schüßel meißtens gehen, abgebildet. sie gehen in wald und auf die berg die wachsende süße
frucht Pytahaya zu sammlen. sie ist inwendig schön roth, außwendig hat sie eine haarige stachliche schaal wie N. 1
der saame aber ist wie zu sehen oben N. 2.

The Changing Patterns of Everyday Life

The neophytes who lived at the missions continued to practice many of the skills that they had used before Europeans came to America. The men often hunted with bows and arrows during their free time. Other Indians spent many hours fishing from the streams and the shoreline. Most neophyte women collected shellfish and wild plants to prepare traditional recipes.

Many of the wild nuts that Indians ate, such as acorns, had to be soaked in fresh water and ground into powder to remove poisonous substances. Some kinds of shellfish, such as abalone, had to be pounded with stones before they could be cooked. To grind and pound their food, the neophyte women used traditional grinding tools, such as cylinder-shaped pestles. They also used rounded stones called mortars, which had deep, hole-like depressions.

Most traditional native cooking took place over an open flame. Many kinds of food were grilled, steamed, or smoked. Some natives used stone griddles. Many dishes were boiled in stone or pottery bowls. Most Californian Indians also knew how to cook food using baskets and hot rocks.

Foods such as corn, beans, wheat, and beef, which the Indians grew and raised, were added to what was already a rich diet. The plentiful wild resources meant that, if the crops failed, there was still usually enough food to eat.

◄ *Native Americans continued to hunt and gather traditional foods after they moved into the missions. The Indian women from Baja California, in this painting by Ignacio Tirsch, are harvesting pitahaya, a kind of cactus fruit, which they used in recipes.*

The mission Indians produced many kinds of traditional artwork and crafts. They used native designs to make different types of objects of exceptional strength, practicality, and beauty. They produced an amazing variety of chipped stone and ground-stone tools, including arrowheads, smoking pipes, and knives. Animal skins were used to make clothing and blankets. Bones

These artifacts were found at Mission San Buenaventura. They are made from wood and might have been used as tools for fishing.

could be turned into drills or needles. Bird feathers were used to make arrows, capes, and headdresses. Seashells became bowls, fishhooks, and jewelry. Grass, rushes, and willow shoots were collected and woven into intricate baskets and mats. Wood was transformed into bowls and tools such as arrows. Over time, European-style objects replaced some of these items, although most neophytes retained at least a few of the older types of tools.

The Indian women of San Diego, San Luis Rey, San Juan Capistrano, San Gabriel, and those that lived in the two Quechan missions of La Purísima and San Pedro y San Pablo continued to manufacture pottery as they had before the arrival of the Europeans. To make ceramics, they dug clay out of streambeds and hillsides. After the clay was combined with water and sand, the Indians formed the mixture into long, cigar-shaped pieces. By carefully coiling the pieces together, the Indians produced a wide variety of bowls and jars. A round stone and a wooden paddle were used to smooth the vessel's surfaces. Once the clay pots had completely dried, they were piled together with wood and brush. The women set the stacks of pottery and fuel on fire. After a few hours, the pottery was allowed to cool.

During their free time, many neophytes continued to enjoy traditional kinds of recreation. Some men spent time in sweathouses. These were small structures that were partially buried in the ground. Inside, a small fire produced smoke and heat. Sweathouses were used to cleanse and heal the body. Other neophytes enjoyed traditional gambling games and sports.

Although many Indians adopted European-style clothing, most neophytes continued customs that made them look different from the Spanish colonists. The men's hair was often worn tied up in the back, near the tops of their heads. Both men and women enjoyed wearing braids and jewelry. The items that were popular included

Neophytes often adopted European hairstyles and clothing, as shown here in an image by Ignacio Tirsch of Baja California.

Skirts, such as this replica, and similar garments made from grass or animal hides, were worn by Chumash women.

bone and shell hairpins and beaded necklaces and earrings. Many of the Indians also continued to use tattoos to decorate their faces and bodies.

During the early years, most neophytes lived in traditional-style native homes. The average Indian used a small hut made of poles and brush, bark, or reeds. The houses had circular floor plans and ranged from 10 to 20 feet (3–6 m) in diameter. The leaders sometimes had larger homes that were up to 50 feet (15 m) across. In some native houses, the insides of the walls were lined with low, wooden platforms that served as beds. Other Indians slept on the ground on reed mats. A fire pit was dug in the middle of the room. A hole in the center of the roof allowed light to enter the structure and smoke to escape.

Changes in Men's Lives

Many of the neophyte men worked in the building trades that were introduced by the Franciscans. The first temporary structures were crude, wood-and-brush houses. Buildings made of mud bricks and tiles usually replaced these huts. After a few years, Indian men worked to combine soil, water, and straw to make hundreds of thousands of adobe bricks. At most missions, there were many kinds of new buildings to create, such as houses, churches, offices, warehouses, mills, and hospitals. Other structures included walled orchards, fountains, and dams.

Some of the men became cowboys and shepherds. The larger missions owned thousands of animals, including cattle, goats, horses, mules, sheep, and pigs. These animals provided milk, cheese, and meat, as well as other useful items, such as leather, wool, and horn.

The cowboys, or vaqueros, took care of the mission's horses and cattle. They had to protect these creatures from wild predators, such as wolves, coyotes, and bears. The horses and cattle often stampeded when they heard unexpected sounds, such as thunder. The neophyte vaqueros also had to round up and brand, or mark, the animals with hot irons.

Most of the men who lived in the missions spent time working in the fields as farmers. The only Indians who grew food before the arrival of the missionaries were the Quechan of the Colorado River. Farming was a new activity for all the other nations now living in the mission communities. Every year, there were dozens of types of crops that had to be planted, taken care of, and harvested. The three most important mission crops were wheat, corn, and barley. The missions were famous for their olives, fruit trees, vineyards, and wine.

Every season of the year brought a new set of farming jobs. Everyone had to help to maintain the fields and the systems of aqueducts that brought water to the most important crops. The planting and harvest times required the largest amounts of work. Everyone who lived at the missions during these periods worked in the fields from sunrise to sunset.

There were many other new trades. Mission factories turned out rope, blankets, soap, clothing, furniture, leather, tile, and pottery. Native blacksmiths produced thousands of nails, knives, hinges, and similar items. A small number of talented neophytes worked as full-time artists. They carved wooden and stone statues and painted religious murals and wall decorations.

Nearly every man at the mission was expected to serve part of the time as a soldier. The Indians needed to be prepared to fight if the mission was ever attacked. The role of the Indians in defense was very important because there were so few Spanish soldiers that the king could spare. At first the neophytes fought as they always had. However, the mission guards eventually trained them to use European weapons, such as firearms and cannons, and European tactics, such as cavalry charges.

Many Indian men developed an interest in the elaborate styles of garments worn by the Spaniards. After less than a decade, most of the Native American leaders wore clothing that was similar to those of the settlers. In the years that followed, the rest of the people adopted similar styles.

Changes in Women's Lives

The Indian women also went through many changes in their lifestyle at the missions. A few worked as craft specialists. However, most women took

This painting by Jack S. Williams shows a cutaway view of a neophyte house at the Mission Santa Bárbara. Women took care of children, cleaned the house, and cooked. The woman wearing the blue head scarf stands by an earthen oven used for cooking.

care of their homes and focused on related household jobs, such as child rearing, cleaning, and cooking.

At many of the missions, a few native women worked at small weaving factories. The massive looms produced excellent wool cloth that was used to make clothing and blankets. Unlike the men, the women had few other new jobs available to them.

The mission women spent many hours cleaning their families' small adobe houses and utensils. They used reed and grass brooms or brushes to sweep the floors and scrub their cooking tools. The women were also responsible for washing clothing and blankets. The families hauled their laundry in large baskets to the closest source of running water. Many missions had elaborate stone and tile washing facilities. The cloth objects had to be thoroughly beaten and scrubbed in the water with soap to remove the dirt before being rinsed. The women passed many hours talking to each other as they scrubbed.

Over time, many native women adopted European cooking traditions. Many of the new methods and tools were similar to those that had been used in the past. Most of the cooking was done outdoors. Fist-sized pieces of stone called *manos* were used to grind corn and wheat into flour on slablike pieces of stone called *metates*. These items were often found alongside traditional mortars and pestles. Many mission cooks also adapted European-style metal and ceramic

A native Californian at the Mission San Luis Obispo probably placed corn, wheat, or acorns on this metate, the larger, flat stone, and ground the grains into flour with a smaller, round mano.

pots and pans to fit their needs. This was a major change for Indians living north of San Gabriel. Before the creation of the missions, these people had never used pottery. Almost every home had its own small stove, and several houses often shared large ovens. These devices were easier to use than the traditional roasting pits and hearths.

The neophyte women learned many European techniques to prepare food. For example, they learned the Spanish method for drying and preserving meat. There were many steps required to prepare the meat from cattle. After the men had skinned the animal, the women cut the flesh from the animal's body. The hearts and tongues were often barbecued right away, but the rest of the meat was dried for later use. The Indians cut the meat into long strips. The pieces were dipped in salt and then hung like ribbons from racks. The Indians stored most of the dried meat in a community warehouse. The women chopped apart the bones with axes and hammers to get the marrow that later would be used for cooking.

The Franciscans thought that it was especially important for the neophyte women and girls to wear European-style clothing. Christianity taught that people needed to cover their bodies. The wives and daughters of the Indian community leaders wore the best dresses. Almost everyone else had outfits that looked like those worn by average Spanish colonists. When they went outside, the women usually covered their heads and shoulders with long pieces of cloth or blankets. This custom followed religious traditions that could be traced to the Middle Ages in Spain, where Muslim women were required to cover most of their heads.

Classroom Education

Because the neophytes had to learn about so many new ways of doing things, the missions often seemed like large schools. Most of the learning took

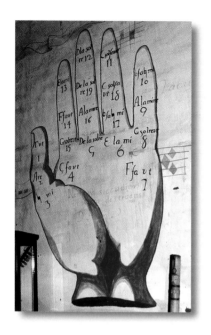

Spanish missionaries taught Native Americans European-style music using a special sign language shown on this giant hand.

place outdoors, through hands-on demonstrations and instructions. However, for certain kinds of lessons, the Franciscans used classrooms. By modern standards, the classrooms were not very well equipped. There were few books, and, most of the time, lessons were taught without a blackboard.

The subjects taught in the classroom included religion, the Spanish language, and music. The students, who included adults and children, generally sat on the floor. The teacher, who was usually a missionary, stood at a large wooden desk. He would read the lessons aloud, and the students would try hard to memorize what he said. When the teacher asked them to, the neophytes were expected to answer questions and repeat memorized sayings.

Many neophytes developed a love for European music. A special system of sign language was created to teach the Indians different musical notes. The Native Americans formed choirs and small bands that sang and played at religious ceremonies and festivals. Some missionaries said that even the neophytes who could hardly understand the newcomers' language showed great talents in playing instruments and singing European-style songs in Latin and Spanish.

Growing Up in a Mission

By the time that they were five, most young people were given chores. Many youths helped to raise smaller animals, such as chickens. Other children protected the crops by driving birds away. Young people also were expected to bring water to their families' houses. The older children helped out with the same jobs that their parents did. They learned their practical education by working with adults.

During the evenings, the children listened to their parents tell folktales. These stories included older Indian legends as well as versions of those that were taught by the colonists. Not only were the stories entertaining, but also they provided life lessons about what was right and what was wrong.

The changes in the native children's lives were not all serious. The neophytes quickly learned how to make their own versions of the colonists' toys. There were wooden hobbyhorses, dolls, and peashooters. Many different European games were popular, including jacks, hopscotch, and blindman's buff. These games were combined with the older traditional gambling games and sports, such as racing.

Religious Life

Religion affected many parts of the neophytes' lives. The beauty of the art and rituals that the Franciscans brought to California made a deep impression on many of the Indians. Although the Native Americans had their own traditional art and ceremonies, none of them had seen anything that was similar to those of the newcomers.

The padres tried to teach their religious views as much as they could to the Native Americans. Over time, the Indians learned that there were prayers, rituals, and ceremonies for almost every aspect of life. Many of the native people loved the church, even when they did not like the newcomers. Not everyone who lived at the missions shared the Franciscans' devotion to Christianity. However, everyone had to go to church and follow other Christian customs.

The houses of worship were very busy places. Religious services were held several times each day. The church was usually the largest and the most beautiful structure in the mission community. Whenever they could, the neophytes and missionaries tried to make improvements on the building. The first churches were often simple boxes made of wood, mud, and grass. Although they were crude by later standards, they were still more impressive than the huts in which the missionaries and the Indians lived. As the neophyte population grew larger, they often built new, bigger churches. By the end of the

Franciscans and Indians worked together to build the missions The materials they used included tile, earthen blocks, and wood.

mission period, magnificent houses of worship had been built. They were fancier than the structures that were used by the colonists and soldiers from Spain or Mexico. Many buildings the Indians erected are still standing today.

The original interiors of the mission churches looked very different from how they look today. When the Indians used them, they did not have any benches. When the priests held religious services, the neophytes stood up or kneeled. The men and boys were found on one side of the church, while the women and girls stood on the other. In the rear of the church, the members of the native choir sang songs in Latin, Spanish, and Indian languages.

During the daylight hours, the major sources of light inside the churches were the small windows in the upper walls. At night, there were hundreds of flickering candles that created mysterious shadows. In the larger churches there were dozens of paintings and statues of saints that covered the walls and altars. Many of the other decorations that were painted on church walls reflected Native American ideas about nature or other tribal traditions. The use of Indian symbols helped the community to feel a sense of ownership for the building. Many neophytes were extremely proud of their church.

Not all the Christian religious ceremonies at the missions were held inside the houses of worship. Some Indian homes had their own altars with crosses, small religious pictures, or even small statues of saints. The Franciscans taught that Christians should begin and end each day with the lighting of candles and family prayers. Many neophytes also wore crosses or carried other similar personal religious objects.

The passage of time in the missions was organized around religious holidays. Most of these occasions were exciting and fun. All work at the mission would stop. The priests led the neophytes in special ceremonies that were often followed by parties that sometimes went on for several days.

The celebrations incorporated many different kinds of events. The religious rituals often included sacred parades. The padres also taught the neophytes that they could make fun of the devil through songs, dances, and even dramatic plays. Many of the neophytes performed traditional native dances. At the larger missions, the neophytes also held bullfights, horse races, and contests between wild bulls and grizzly bears.

Although the padres tried to prevent it, many older Native American religious traditions survived. The Indian people often combined Christian beliefs with native ideas and customs. Many ancient native holidays and rituals were observed in secret.

Many Indians became loyal Roman Catholics. One possible reason that Christianity was so popular was that it provided comfort during a time of many changes and uncertainty. Throughout the missions there were deaths because of new diseases. Even where new illnesses were not a problem, life was filled with dangers. The lack of medical knowledge meant that most people had to put up with a great deal of physical pain. There were so many challenges that it comforted people to think that the angels, the saints, and God were looking after them.

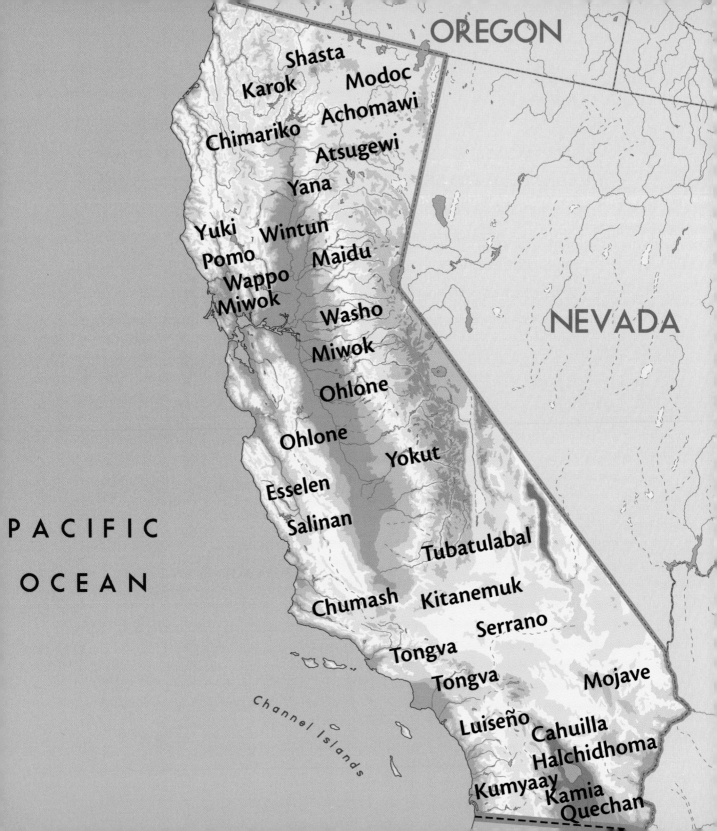

PACIFIC

OCEAN

OREGON

NEVADA

Shasta
Karok
Modoc
Achomawi
Chimariko
Atsugewi
Yana
Yuki
Wintun
Pomo
Maidu
Wappo
Miwok
Washo
Miwok
Ohlone
Ohlone
Yokut
Esselen
Salinan
Tubatulabal
Chumash
Kitanemuk
Serrano
Tongva
Tongva
Mojave
Channel Islands
Luiseño
Cahuilla
Halchidhoma
Kumyaay
Kamia
Quechan

Nonmission Indian Neighbors

Not all the Indians who lived in the regions of California where the Franciscans worked were neophytes. Some natives continued to live outside of the missions. At first, the neophytes represented a small part of the total Native American population. As time passed, the number of gentiles declined in most of Spanish California.

Meetings between the neophytes and the gentiles were common. Every year the Christians were encouraged to travel to their old communities, where they traded and visited with old friends and relatives. The Franciscans counted on these visits to bring new Indians into the missions. Records indicate that this approach to spreading the word about the missions led to dramatic growth in the Franciscan settlements throughout California.

Sometimes the meetings between the neophytes and the gentiles were not so friendly. Some mission Indians used their trips away from the Franciscan outposts to attack old enemies. Sometimes the gentiles attacked the Christians. The soldiers from the military outposts were usually called to help end the fights.

When the Indians became Christians, they agreed to work and live for the rest of their lives as part of the Spanish community. Everyone who lived at the missions depended on everyone else for their survival. The missionaries

◄ *This map of California shows the locations of the different Native American nations. The California Indians were divided into many groups, each with their own unique languages and customs.*

taught the Indians many skills that were very valuable to enemy gentile Indians. No one, including the European colonists, was allowed to drop all his responsibilities and move away. If a person did such a thing, he was considered to be a traitor to the king and to God.

Walls did not surround the missions, and there were rarely any soldiers or Franciscans around to keep an eye on someone who wanted to leave. A small part of the neophyte population did run away to live with the gentiles. The mission Indian leaders and the soldiers sometimes tried to follow and capture them. Most of the time they failed. However, many of the runaway neophytes eventually came back to their mission homes. It seems that however difficult it was for them to live at the missions, life among the gentiles was even more difficult. A very small number of people ran away repeatedly. They were either punished or were forced to spend time in jail.

Native Responses to Life at the Missions

The missions represented many different kinds of experiences for the California Indians. In some regions, the benefits of the new ways seemed to outweigh the problems. The missions built for the Chumash, the Salinans, and the Luiseños enjoyed prosperity and peace. Before the end of the mission era in 1835, these nations showed deep commitment to supporting the Spanish government and were enthusiastic followers of Christianity. By contrast, the Ohlone, Kumeyaay, Tongva, and Quechan missions were particularly troubled. There most of the Indian people either rejected the missions or showed serious doubts about the value of friendship with the newcomers.

Some Native American leaders fought the missionaries. Olleyquotequiebe was a Quechan leader who drove the Franciscans and the Spanish army from his homeland. His people controlled an important river crossing on the road that connected California to central Mexico. In 1775, Spanish missionaries and soldiers reached the Quechan homeland on the Colorado River. They asked Olleyquotequiebe to allow them to pass through his peoples' territory.

The Quechan leader quickly made friends with the newcomers. He wanted an alliance with the Spanish army, and he was willing to trade land and to permit them to cross the river to gain their friendship. Olleyquotequiebe even

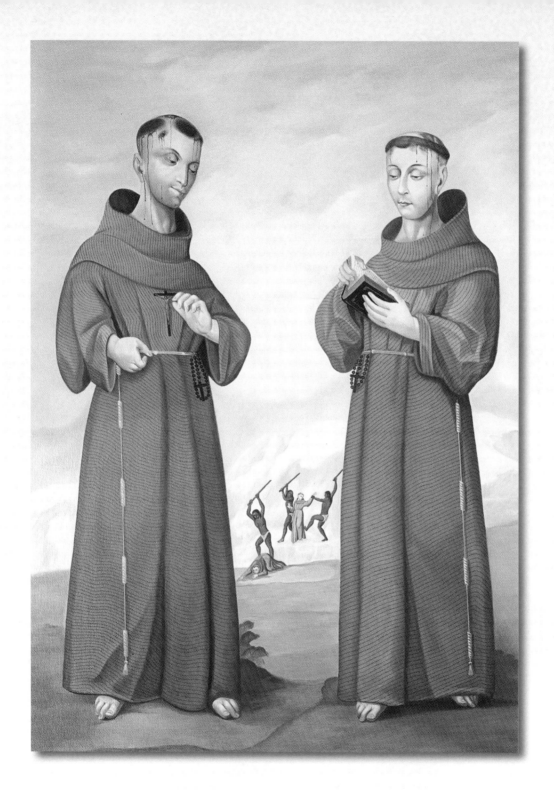

went to Mexico City, where the bishop of the capital made Olleyquotequiebe a Christian. The European priests gave him the new name, Salvador Palma.

After he returned to his people, Olleyquotequiebe asked the Spaniards for missionaries and soldiers. He wanted the newcomers to provide his people with trade goods and military support. In 1779, Franciscans began to live with the Quechan. They soon created two missions known as La Purísima Concepción and San Pedro y San Pablo at the Yuma Crossing.

After less than two years, it became obvious that the Spaniards could not keep their promises. Olleyquotequiebe and the other leaders of the Quechan decided to get rid of the newcomers. In 1781, they destroyed the missions, the Spanish settlements, and either killed or captured every one of the foreigners. For the next three years, Olleyquotequiebe defeated army after army that was sent to fight him. For the rest of the colonial period, California's land route to Mexico was closed. By keeping the Spaniards from sending supplies and people on this route, Olleyquotequiebe influenced the entire history of the frontier. Although few people know his name, he remains a hero to the Quechan nation and a symbol of Indian resistance to foreign invasion.

Not all the people who fought the European soldiers and missionaries were men. One of the most remarkable people of the mission era was an Indian holy woman and leader named Toypurina. Her life reflects the complexity of the relationship that existed between the Native Americans and the newcomers.

Toypurina was ten years old when the Spaniards first arrived to establish Mission San Gabriel in 1771. Her people, the Tongva Nation, lived around

Father Francisco Garcés and Father Juan Antonio Barrneche were two of the four padres that were killed in what became known as the Yuma massacre of 1781.

what is today Los Angeles. By 1785, she had become an important religious leader to those that opposed the mission. She formed an alliance with some of the neophytes to kill the priests and destroy the mission. The soldiers discovered her plans, and she was arrested. At her trial, Toypurina bravely declared that she opposed the Spaniards because they were stealing her people's land and stopping her people from worshiping in the old way.

After she was found guilty, Toypurina was sent into exile at Mission San Carlos, near Monterey. The people who lived there accepted Toypurina as a

Mission San Carlos (above), *near Monterey, California, was the place where the Spaniards sent Toypurina after she plotted to destroy the Mission San Gabriel and to kill its padres. W. Alexander created this picture from a sketch made by J. Sykes.*

member of their community. Eventually, she became a Christian, fell in love with one of the soldiers at the mission, and married him. After Toypurina's marriage, her husband was assigned to guard the new Ohlone mission at San Juan Bautista, and she moved with him to the outpost. Toypurina died of natural causes as a member of the Spanish, and not the Native American, community. She gave birth to four children. One of her sons became a soldier, and one of her daughters married a soldier.

The story of Toypurina shows how some of the people who fought the new settlers changed their minds. Other Indians who lived with the Franciscans seemed to have adapted well to their new lives at the missions. They were proud of their close relationship with the padres.

One of the best-known native leaders to side with the newcomers was Pablo Tac, a Luiseño. He was born at Mission San Luis Rey in about 1820. As a young man, Tac went to Rome to become a priest. While in Italy, he wrote a short history of his people and their life with the missionaries. Tac's words make it clear that he was grateful to have lived at the mission, and that he accepted and even loved his new way of life. Sadly, Tac died before he could complete his training as a priest. He was never able to serve his people.

The Mission Heritage

For better or for worse, the missions changed California's native world forever. Despite the problems that existed, the missions represented a Franciscan-Indian partnership, which offered some hope for the future of California's first inhabitants. Elsewhere in North America, the Indians were usually murdered or driven away by Europeans who did not accept that the Native Americans were human beings.

Even if there had never been any missions, Europeans and all the troubles that they brought to the Indians would have come to California eventually. Many of the native people realized that the missions were not the fundamental cause of their troubles.

The missions were eliminated between 1834 and 1835. The era of the Mexican ranchos that followed saw the Christian natives stripped of their property. Under the rule of the United States there were even worse horrors. The California gold rush, which began in 1849, brought tens of thousands of ruthless fortune hunters to the region. Although there was little gold to be found in the mission areas, the immigrants soon found other resources that they could steal. In 1850, Governor Peter Burnett ordered that all the remaining Native Americans in California should be exterminated. That same year, Captain Nathaniel Lyon of the U.S. Cavalry attacked the Pomos of

This photo shows Chumash Indians during the difficult period after the missions period had ended. ➤

northern California. He proved that the new government was willing to accept the murder of innocent Native American men, women, and children.

We will never know what might have happened if the California missions had been allowed to continue. Based on events that took place in other regions where Franciscans worked, it is likely that the problems of disease would have ended gradually. The native population of the missions would probably have grown. Over time, they would have become a part of the larger Spanish-speaking world.

San Francisco Solano

San Rafael Arcángel

Presidio
de San
Francisco

San José

Santa Clara de Asís

Pueblo de San José

Santa Cruz

Pueblo de Branciforte

San Juan Bautista

Presidio de
San Carlos
de Monterey

San Carlos Borromeo
de Carmelo

Nuestra Señora de la Soledad

San Antonio de Padua

San Miguel Arcángel

San Luis Obispo de Tolosa

La Purísima Concepción

Santa Inés

Santa Bárbara

Presidio de Santa Bárbara

San Fernando
Rey de España

San Buenaventura

Pueblo de
Los Angeles

San Gabriel
Arcángel

San Juan
Capistrano

San Luis Rey
de Francia

Presidio de San Diego

San Diego
de Alcalá

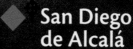

Glossary

adobe (uh-DOH-bee) An earthen block that is made with mud and straw or grass.

allies (A-lyz) People or countries that support one another.

Alta California (AL-tuh kah-lih-FOR-nee-uh) The area along the west coast of America where the Spaniards built missions, today known as the state of California.

Baja California (BAH-hah ka-lih-FOR-nee-uh) The region of Lower California that today corresponds to the Mexican states of Baja California and Baja California Sur.

barren (BAR-en) Producing little in the way of plants or crops.

brand (BRAND) A kind of iron pole with a design that is used to mark animals, such as cattle.

clan (KLAN) A group of people who are part of the same larger family.

conquistadors (kon-KEES-tuh-dorz) Spanish soldiers who explored and conquered large areas of the Americas between 1500 and 1600.

curacy (KYU-run-see) A community that is under the control of a priest or religious official.

descendants (dih-SEN-dents) People who are born of a certain family or group.

desolate (DEH-soh-let) A place with few inhabitants, or appearing to be without life.

dispute (dih-SPYOOT) To argue or fight with another.

doctrinas (dok-TREEN-uhz) Native settlements where Indians were given more control.

expedition (ek-spuh-DIH-shun) A trip for a special purpose, such as exploring or conquering a new land.

gentile (JEN-tyl) A word used by missionaries for Native Americans who were not Christians.

griddle (GRID-uhl) A large, flat pan used to fry food.

loom (LOOM) A machine that is used for weaving yarn into cloth.

manos (MAH-nohs) Grinding tools made from stone that are used to make cornmeal and similar powders.

metates (meh-TAH-tays) Grinding tools made from stone that are used to make cornmeal and similar powders.

mortars (MOR-turz) Circular holes in rocks that were used to crack nuts and grind seeds into flour.

neophytes (NEE-uh-fyts) Native Americans who became Christians.

pestles (PEH-sulz) A tool used to pound something into powder.

privileges (PRIV-lij) Special rights or favors.

rancho (RAN-choh) A large farm for raising cattle, horses, or sheep. In California this term is mostly associated with larger cattle farms.

reducción (reh-duk-see-OHN) A kind of mission community in which people are drawn together from other areas.

rituals (RIH-choo-ul) A religious ceremony.

secularization (seh-kyuh-luh-rih-ZAY-shun) The process by which a mission community goes from being controlled by the priests to being controlled by the Indians.

social structure (SOH-shul STRUHK-chur) A social system that separates people into groups and gives them certain jobs.

utopia (yoo-TOH-pee-uh) An ideal community in which everyone is treated fairly and is happy.

vaqueros (vah-KER-ohs) The Spanish word for cowboys.

Resources

There are many places where you can learn more about mission Indians. The following lists provide information about some of the more important resources.

Books:

Webb, Edith. *Indian Life at the Old Missions.* Los Angeles: Wayside Press, 1952.

Williams, Jack S. *The Chumash of California.* New York: Rosen Publishing, 2002.

Young, Stanley, Sally B. Woodbridge, and Melba Levick. *Missions of California.* San Francisco: Chronicle Books, 1998.

Museums:

La Purísima Mission State Historic Park. 2295 Purísima Road, Lompoc, California, 93436. (805) 733-3713.

This park, located on the outskirts of Lompoc, California, contains buildings preserved from one of the most important and elaborate of the missions.

Web Sites:

Due to the changing nature of Internet links, PowerKids Press has developed an online list of Web sites related to the subject of this book. This site is updated regularly. Please use this link to access the list:

www.powerkidslinks.com/pcm/indian/

Index

About The Authors

Dr. Jack Stephen Williams has worked as an archaeologist and historian on various research projects in the United States, Mexico, South America, and Europe. Williams has a particular interest in the Native Americans and early colonization of the Southwest and California. He holds a doctoral degree in anthropology from the University of Arizona and has written numerous books and articles. Williams lives in San Diego, California, with his wife, Anita G. Cohen-Williams, and his daughter, Louise.

Thomas L. Davis, M. Div, M.A., was first introduced to the California missions in 1957 by his grandmother. He began to collect books, photos, and any other materials about the missions. Over the years, he has assembled a first-class research library about the missions and Spanish North America, and he is a respected authority in his field. After ten years of working in the music business, Davis studied for the Catholic priesthood and was ordained for service in Los Angeles, California. Ten years as a Roman Catholic priest saw Friar Thom make another life change. He studied at U.C.L.A. and California State University, Northridge, where he received his M.A. in history. He is a founding member of the California Mission Studies Association and teaches California and Latin American history at College of the Canyons, Santa Clarita, California. Davis lives in Palmdale, California, with his wife, Rebecca, and son, Graham.